# Aspirational Thoughts Inspirational Images

AN ART GALLERY
AND TEACHER,
A PHOTOGRAPHY EXHIBIT
AND MENTOR

FRANK McKINNEY

## ALSO BY FRANK McKINNEY

*Adversitology: Overcoming Adversity When You're Hanging on by a Thread* (Inspirational Memoir)

*Aspire! How to Create Your Own Reality and Alter Your DNA* (Mindset)

*The Other Thief* (Christian Romance)

*The Tap* (Spirituality)

*Burst This! Frank McKinney's Bubble-Proof Real Estate Strategies* (Real Estate)

*Dead Fred, Flying Lunchboxes, and the Good Luck Circle* (Young Reader Fantasy)

*Frank McKinney's Maverick Approach to Real Estate Success: How You Can Go from a $50,000 Fixer-Upper to a $100 Million Mansion* (Real Estate)

*Make It BIG! 49 Secrets for Building a Life of Extreme Success* (Philosophy)

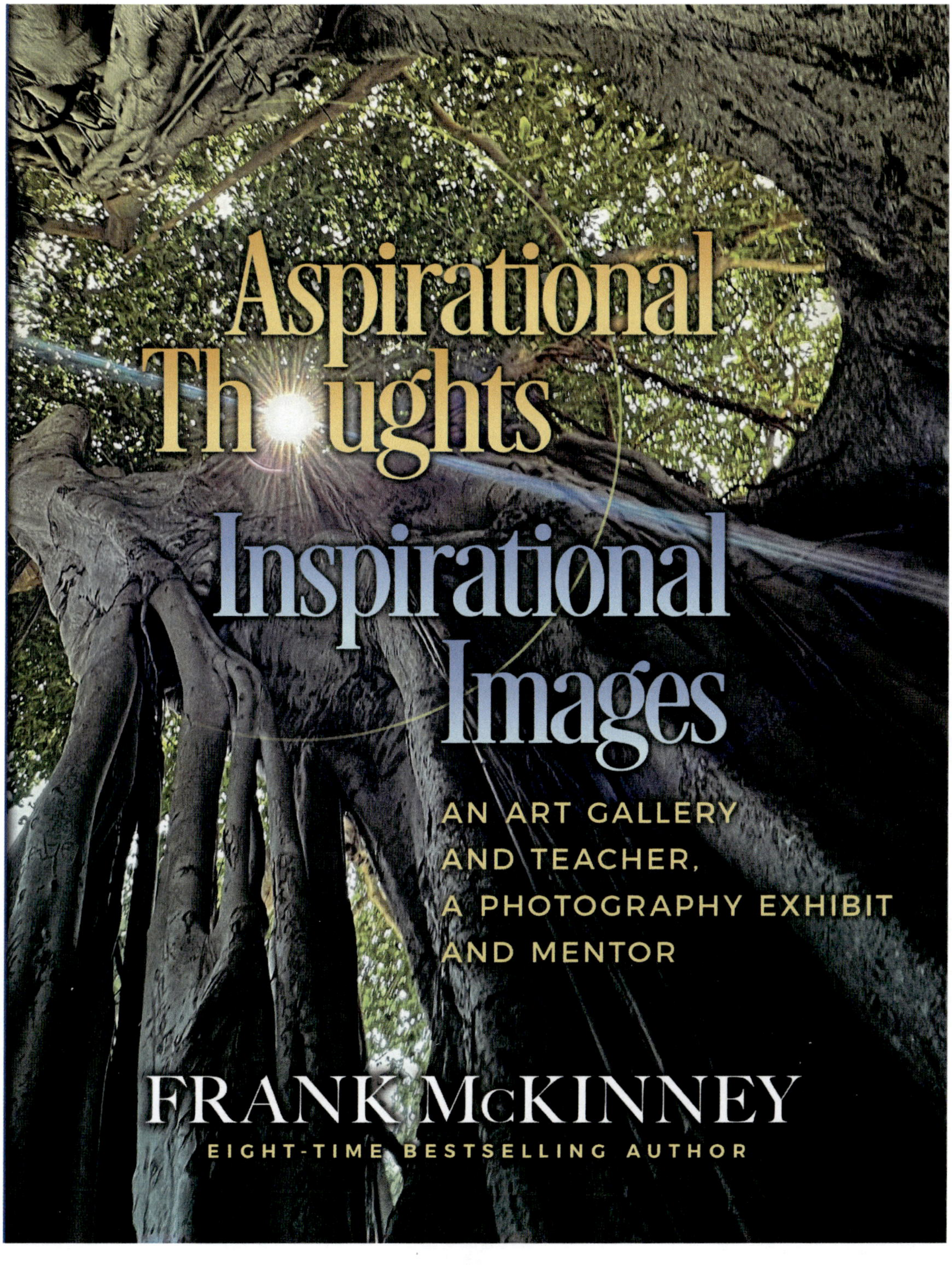


Caring House
BOOKS
FLORIDA

*Aspirational Thoughts • Inspirational Images: An Art Gallery and Teacher, A Photography Exhibit and Mentor*



For permissions requests, speaking inquiries, and bulk order purchase options,
e-mail pamela@frank-mckinney.com.

Caring House Books
P.O. Box 388, Boynton Beach, Florida 33425

ISBN: 978-1-7362376-8-7

1st edition, April 2024

Printed in the United States of America

Cover and interior design: Robert Mott for RobertMottDesigns.com
Photography: Frank McKinney
Author photo: Nilsa McKinney

# DEDICATION

*To my other Dad, "Ern-Burn," Ernesto Colon.*
*Ernie taught me how to be a husband and father,*
*not by spoken instruction, but through images retained*
*by observing his love for his daughter*
*(and my wife, Nilsa) and the rest of his family.*

# CONTENTS

Introduction . . . . . 1
Action . . . . . 7
Introspect . . . . . 33
Laugh . . . . . 55
Breathe . . . . . 81
Legacy . . . . . 107
Death . . . . . 135
Risk . . . . . 161
Hope . . . . . 189
God . . . . . 215
Love . . . . . 243
Acknowledgments . . . . . 269
About Frank McKinney . . . . . 273
Other Bestselling Offerings From Frank McKinney . . . . . 275

# INTRODUCTION

In approaching the composition of *Aspirational Thoughts • Inspirational Images* I saw the undertaking as this enormous 2,000-piece jigsaw puzzle, not only in 3D, but by adding a 4th dimension.

Unfortunately, the pieces weren't conveniently dumped onto a coffee table in my living room, as they were scattered all over creation, or better yet, all over my "creations." The pieces were needles hidden in dozens of haystacks, where I was the one who stacked the hay long, long ago! No two elements were the same. Some pieces were brand new in 2024, and some of the pieces I hadn't seen in over 26 years.

To begin to put together the complex puzzle, I went back through all eight of my prior bestsellers, including content found in original manuscripts that didn't make it into the final books. I also scrolled back five years on social media, re-read certain webpages of mine and even watched/listened to recordings of when I was interviewed to revisit much of what I've written or said—with some new material created as recently as the day before this book went to print in 2024!

The first puzzle piece I picked up was a marked-up draft of the original manuscript for my first book, which I began writing in 1998. And I kept gathering the pieces, all the way through to my most recent writings and interviews into 2024.

To assemble the first parts of the puzzle, I collected a whopping 1,112 initial thoughts, quotes, soundbites, and ideas that could possibly be considered for inclusion in *Aspirational Thoughts • Inspirational Images.* I then cut that total down to 261 of the most impactful, the absolute best of the best, the shiniest of all the gems. The final written elements of this book are all meat, no fluff, getting directly to the point with none of the superfluous build-up found in many typical chapter books.

For the remaining parts of the puzzle, I culled through 898 photographs that I've taken more recently over the past five years, as I have begun to enjoy photography, primarily nature photography. These images were whittled down to 135 that paired perfectly with the written words.

All the pieces of the puzzle have now been combined and put together into 10 meditative categories found in the book you are now holding: *Action, Introspect, Laugh, Breathe, Legacy, Death, Risk, Hope, God,* and *Love.*

And here is the breakthrough reason why I composed a book in this manner. Really, a whole new way to read, retain, then implement your favorite ideas, thoughts, and quotes.

But first I must take you back to your early childhood ...

Do you remember how you learned to recall your first, and oh-so-impactful, written words? Probably not, but I'm sure you'll recollect those early picture books. These were thin, hardcover books that might have had a cute illustration of a dog, cat, or horse on the left-hand page, and on the opposite page there was a large-font word to coincide, like *DOG, CAT, HORSE,* etc. Your mom, dad, or teacher would have you say the word, then have you look at the image to retain that word and its meaning or application.

The image helped you learn the word!

I don't know about you, but when I read something impactful, I pause. I might underline the sentence or two, I might close my eyes and ponder it or decide to look out the window to concentrate on its meaning, or I might just stare at something while I try to interpret it. We do these things because the subconscious mind wants to find a place to file and store what we just read for future retrieval and reliance.

With *Aspirational Thoughts • Inspirational Images,* using wonderment, spontaneity, and serenity, you are encouraged to reflect upon the awe-inspiring images in conversation with unconventional written wisdom.

Watch ... as the images help you remember then act upon the words!

It's a scientific fact that we retain critical information better when we associate it with an image.

*Aspirational Thoughts • Inspirational Images* can be viewed as three distinct books in one. In addition to its intended use, if you simply enjoy images of nature and other beautiful things, forget the quotes, and just enjoy the book of photography. If you're not into that kind of thing, and just love reading, then by all means dive into the 10,011 aspirational words, and try *not* to be distracted by the images. I bet you can't!

Finally, for the 4th dimension (and this is going to be really fun!) I wanted you to be able to "peek behind the curtain," between the pages. In a mini behind-the-scenes documentary, you'll hear in my own words: the background, perspective, color commentary, and even humorous side stories on certain breathtaking images. *What's the story behind that image, Frank? Where in the world did you take that photo?* At the end of each chapter, you'll find a QR code. Simply scan that code and be taken to a private video where you'll be amazed and entertained as I narrate while random images tell their stories!

Listen to the images

**Introduction**

Allow *Aspirational Thoughts • Inspirational Images*
to be your private art gallery and teacher,
your personal photography exhibit and mentor.

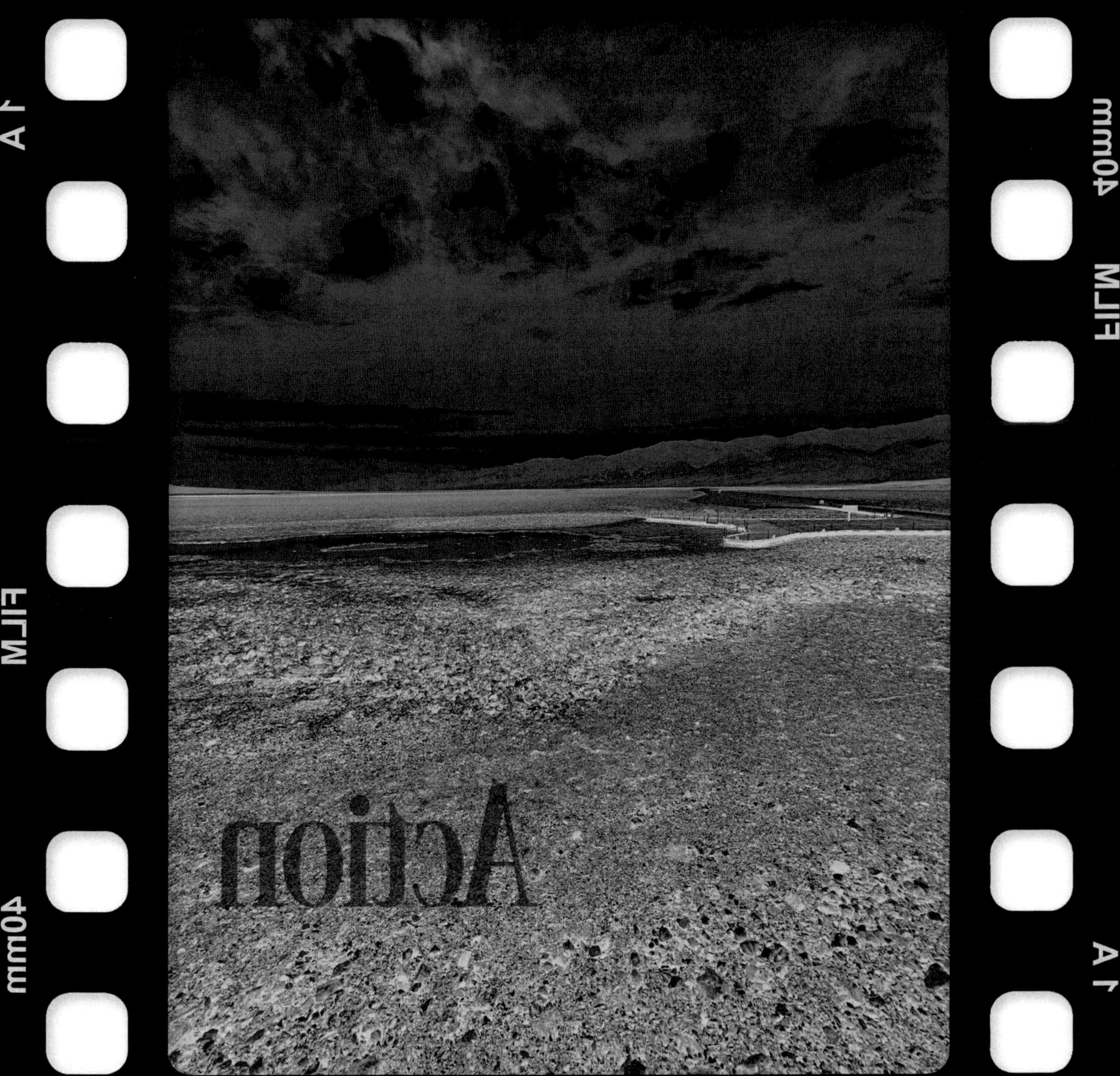
Action

ACTION
Action

**If you're gonna have regrets
(which you will),
regret what you did,
not what you didn't do.**

Be one of you instead of one of them.

"Work smarter, not harder." I despise that saying. What if you worked harder *and* smarter?

Time moves, so you better move with it.

1100

Here's the secret to discipline:
it's easier when it's in service to an aspiration.

Don't let over-googling, over-pondering,
over-spreadsheeting, or overthinking get in the way
of killing the person you are today
to become the person you aspire to be.

When I get an idea in my head that I want to pursue I will decide to do it on impulse, in the moment. That's when an impulse seed is firmly planted. And once I decide, nothing's going to get in my way. However, I do put the initial thought through the "impulse filter" to quickly learn if it's constructive or destructive. You would think being able to tell the two apart would be easy—yet, for me, sometimes it's not.

Think fast. Act faster.

Practicality allows you to execute what your creativity and passion create.

Focus on one thing and get great at it.

We feel most alive when we experience extremes for the first time, in our pursuit to live the dichotomies found in life, not by merely existing in the "comfort corridor."

Instead of asking, *Why is it this way?*

Ask, *What can I do to help?*

Live your inside on your outside.

ADVERSITOLOGY
PLEASE HELP
OVERCOME
ADVERSITY!

You won't strengthen your compassion "muscle" by serving Thanksgiving dinner at the soup kitchen once a year or contributing $10 to a friend's GoFundMe campaign.

Never stand still.
It is not your desire to maintain a level of past achievements. Maintenance is never a goal.

Compassion without action is a waste of emotion.

Success requires the disciplined application
of effort through time.

Commit to saying yes more than no.
Whenever you're faced with a life-advancing decision,
make your automatic response a life-affirming *yes*.
See how much richer your life is as a result.

Act with integrity:
Live up to your own idea
of who you are.

Nothing will happen
until you take action.

Motivation and inspiration don't last.
They lack the deep conscious and
subconscious feeling created
when you aspire to something mighty.

While you might lose motivation and inspiration,
aspiration is sacred.

Take proactive measures to overcome any form of adversity. Wallowing is easy. Action is hard. Execution is tough. NEVER sit still in your adversity; accept it and face it down.

Take your ATV out for a spin today: be authentic, transparent, and vulnerable!

The snooze button didn't exist until 1956. For me, it still doesn't.

Aspirations are not resolutions or goals;
they are far bigger and more meaningful.
They are the inner drivers found deep in the soul
that will take you to new levels of success,
quality of life, and love far beyond
what you could ever imagine.

You don't have to change. You can simply take what's
already inside you and reignite or redirect it.

Don't overthink; instead, overdo.

Listen to the images

Action

Introspect

Introspect
INTROSPECT

**I'll never get old. I'll stay young forever. While "me" may age—yes, my body gets older, the tissues of my brain age, but *thought,* the "I," is ageless. Our thoughts don't have to age. You may suppose they should, but they don't have to. Age will bring enlightenment, efficiency, and intelligence, but the process of cognitive and creative thought that leads to behavioral action doesn't have to age. Unlike the lines on your face, the grey in your hair, the pain in your knees, or the pace of your day, your thoughts can be as youthful as you choose.**

**Reality isn't what's "out there"; it's what you let "in here."**

Introspection is taking the time to figure yourself out. It's the ability to turn inside and thoroughly examine yourself with an honest x-ray of your successes and mistakes.

Problems or impediments to your aspirations don't exist; what exists is an artificially inflated evaluation of the importance of *things*. The simpler the things, the deeper the appreciation.

It's not that you want money: you want what you perceive money will do for you.

AVISO
LLAMADAS
TELEFONICAS
PODRIAN SER
GRARADAS Y
MONITOREADAS
TELEPHONE
CALLS MAY BE
RECORDED AND
MONITORED
01
03

You will experience only two types of adversity in your life: self-inflicted (consequential) and external (innocent).

How many of us imprison our dreams, our goals, our gifts, and our aspirations behind walls we build, brick by brick, based upon our fears or feeling like we're inadequate or unqualified?

Too many of us tend to talk ourselves out of sound, intuitive decisions. We ponder, we equivocate, we second-guess ourselves out of what turns out to have been the right course.

Having a lot of money, being rich, will give you two things in absolute abundance: relief and comfort. All the relief and comfort you can imagine. But notice what's missing ...

There are four "able" requirements for any constructive objective: They must be quantifiable, measurable, manageable, and tangible. (Don't quibble with an "ible" ...)

As slowly as the Fall leaves change, the Winter ice freezes,
the Spring buds blossom, the Summer sand scorches,
so will come the change you seek. But it will come.

It's better to be overrated than underrated.

The harder you battle something,
the more entwined you become.
You fight it, you empower it, period.

FORD

My addictive personality, or my tendency toward one, has made me a fortune. I'm fully aware that the addictive personality traits are still there and will be until I die. The key for me is to continue to shine a light on the "whys." I ask myself, *Are you really addicted to* _______ (fill in the bank), *or is it addicted to you because 'it' knows of your predisposition?* If it's a harmful addiction I quickly realize I wouldn't be addicted to something that would hurt me (or those I love), but the thing is addicted to ME. I then refuse to over-identify with the thing (the demon—everyone fights them).

There's a constructive difference between having narcissistic tendencies and being a narcissist.

Disidentify: You give adversity as much power as you are using to wage war against it. When you renounce something, you're tied to it through the energy you use to fight it.

Any strength that's overused and unchecked becomes an obstacle rather than an asset.

A cycle will take you around in circles, repeating behavior ingrained through attachments that were broken only when a new attachment took its place.

The only thing that stays the same in life is change.

NOW I LAY ME DOWN TO SLEEP
I PRAY THEE LORD MY SOUL TO KEEP

What I would call vision and aspiration are what far too many call dreams. Have the vision to see a dream as something you can and will turn into reality.

Are you always focused on becoming, achieving, and attaining, or alternatively chasing some new thrill or pleasure? Do you believe that if you acquire more things you will become more fulfilled, good enough, or psychologically complete? Are you waiting for a man or woman to give meaning to your life? If so, it's a maddening cycle that will *never* end.

Dreams are something we have when we sleep. Have aspirations that violently wake you that you make come true!

There are over 10,000,000 colors in the world.
Heck, there have been over 200 Crayola crayon colors alone!
God gave us millions of colors for an infinite number of reasons.
One of them is color releases creativity.
Colors represent a trigger that detonates a creative explosion
in the mind and the firing of synapses as one,
authoring their own new reality. Colors amplify creativity.

Thrills and excitement are not happiness.
They are thrills and excitement.
True happiness is uncaused.

Life is a beautiful mystery.

If we are fortunate, 97 percent of our ordinary life
is spent pursuing the extraordinary 3 percent.
Enjoy the 97 percent and recognize and adore
the 3 percent as extraordinarily golden moments.

Who needs Artificial Intelligence
when you can have the real thing?

The mind wills the body to do what the mind wants
and what the body does not want.

ATII: just making sure we remember why we're here ...

Listen to the images

Introspect

# LAUGH

Laugh

CAUTION
THIN ICE

**If all the world's a stage, then I want a brighter spotlight.**

**There are too many starving artists out there and plenty of one-hit-wonder success stories. Don't be either.**

Women tend to see things in 3D.

Men only see in 2D (or 1D if you're really shallow ;) )

There's no harm in enhancing the truth

with your own take on it.

Each day you are on the concert stage of life,

so you'd better make it rock!

If during your lifetime at least a few people aren't
shaking their heads and asking,
"What in the world was he or she thinking?"
you are playing way too small.

Resist the temptation to act like an adult.
Let the kid inside of you come out.
There you'll find a sense of humor and irreverence.

Laugh often ... and make sure you're
able to laugh at yourself.

Drugs amplify. Drugs make less.

Drugs amplify natural highs and make less natural lows.

There's a reason it's called *natural.*

Reaching the pot of gold feels great for a while,

but happiness, real joy, and enlightenment is what is experienced

while sliding down the rainbow.

When I was younger, I was the kind of guy who thought he could throw stuff out of hotel windows into the pool and get away with it. Well, actually, I *did* get away with it.

I'm happy to be a living science experiment, a human Petri dish, when it comes to anything that will allow me to exceed the known limits of my body. It's on you to amplify your essence and create your brand.

Products or services can't speak for themselves. You've got to be the P. T. Barnum, the carnival barker, the ringmaster, the human megaphone that entices people into the show.

MOTEL 6

*Frank, at your age you scripted, wrote, directed, and starred in a stunt where you rode a motorcycle through a burning image of the cover of your seventh book in six genres (a cover you also designed). You did all this while being lit on fire and delivering lines to a movie camera in one take ... no re-dos. Why in God's name isn't that enough?*

Sometimes you just gotta run up the aisle and take the wheel, whether or not you know exactly how to drive a 30-ton bus!

I believe that had God not sent Nilsa to me I'd likely be dead or living in a beat-up old Airstream trailer somewhere in the backwoods of West Virginia, wearing overalls, chewing tobacco, smelling like motor oil, and married to the bearded lady from the circus.

When you stick your head in the sand,
what sticks out of the ground?
Your ass, to get kicked!

Indian
MOTORCYCLE
SINCE 1901

Frank's fly-fishing tips: Use a bobber.
Use sausage and cheese as bait.
Forget the fly rod.
Remember your lucky fishing hat.

I'm a lot less exciting than I look.
I'm really a nerd in sheep's clothing.

"Have you always had your faith, Frank?"
My answer: "Yes, but sometimes I have forgotten how to practice it."

For Nilsa, being married to me is like putting on
a beautiful flame-retardant Dior dress each morning,
and with a rosary in one hand and a scotch in the other,
strapping yourself into a rocket-fueled rollercoaster,
knowing that when the ride hits 100 mph the cosmos will switch off
gravity and the coaster will careen off into space,
leaving you wondering (again) if you'll land in a black hole
or end up in a new, unpopulated Garden of Eden.

# Trees and Yugos are art.

RESTING
EVAN Z.
SON OF
ZIEGLER & AMANDA
BRADYCAMP
NOV. 22, 1874

Welcome to nature's IMAX theater.
Enjoy the show: Death Valley.

It's important to know that your role models don't have to be "real" people: if you feel that emulating Willy Wonka, Superman, Robin Hood, Wonder Woman, or Black Panther will help you pursue your aspirations, do it.

So many people clench their hands at 10 and 2, driving themselves straight to a job from hell. Hell on earth, anyway.

If Jesus were here in our world today with
studded and ripped jeans, colorful jackets, long purple hair,
and a Yugo, how would he act; what would he do?

I'm 16 going on 60, or is it 60 going on 16?
Either way, I'm never growing up.

Listen to the images

Laugh

1A
40mm
FILM
Breathe

BREATHE
Breathe

**Be selective in silence.**

**More changes take place in the mind than in reality.**

Peeling away the things that tie you to your past
can make you feel extraordinarily vulnerable and raw.

The acceptance of one's life and how it has unfolded ...
or how it continues to unfold ...
that is where you find true peace.

The vital importance of health:
without it, we are nothing.

Creativity is akin to the sound of opening a soda can:
a veritable explosion of light and sound
and color in the synapses.

Life tends to reward the brave: those who develop
a deep understanding that we should live with and
embrace the contrasts presented by life
are rewarded beyond common measure.

Your net worth is not your self-worth.

Creativity and ingenuity are the
two primary qualities
that are exponentially rewarded.

Go with your intuition, never
with your runaway mind.

Avoid vices and unhealthy temptations
as they suck the life out of progress and success.

Become aware of the reason you have allowed an adversity
into your life and, more important, how you have come to see it
as some indomitable, uncontrollable force.
It is through understanding the obsession,
and your dependency on it, that it slowly disappears.

What sets you apart is still inside you,
but you've suppressed it for so freaking long
that it may take a while to dig it out.

People can have good self-esteem but an underdeveloped ego:
they can think well of themselves while lacking an accurate
sense of their value. Most people fall into the category
of good self-esteem yet underdeveloped ego.

Accentuate and amplify your essence.

When you combine a healthy ego with empathy you have a magic formula that will counter any potential narcissism and allow you to bring your gifts out to benefit the world.

Do less to enjoy more. Simplify.

Never lose the little girl or boy inside, for that is where creativity and ingenuity are found.

Happiness is hope realized for the moment, then living with that flowing moment every moment.

The rational mind dissolves, disintegrates,
disappears when confronted with severe adversity.
This is denialism.
Denialism is simply the mind's way
of protecting itself from an uncomfortable
or threatening situation.

Every success contains its adversities.
Be grateful for both.

Motivation washes off and goes down the drain with the soap at night. Inspiration lasts about as long as a bad sunburn. But Aspiration can alter your DNA, allowing you to create the reality you want.

Draw strength from criticism
and predictions of doom.

Life will always be a mosaic while I (we, you) struggle to tame the mercurial side.

It's in those moments of deafening solitude, when it seems there's no answer to your prayers, that you need to be most attentive and proactive, not shut down and self-centered.

Strive to toggle between right and left brain in nanoseconds.

There is no perfection in faith; there's only practice.
Lots and lots of practice.

Imagine that your mind is a clear sky, and that life's joys and small pleasures are puffy white clouds and sunny days, while adversities are dark clouds. These ominous clouds darken the sky, issue thunder and lightning, cause destructive storms and chaos, frighten people. Yet the biggest, darkest thunderclouds all pass. All clouds pass, including the happy ones, as will adversity. By its very nature, adversity is fleeting (in the grand scheme of an entire life) and temporary.

Savor everything. Cling to nothing.

Listen to the images

Breathe

Legacy

LEGACY
Legacy

**Your personal brand should be such an original, unique, and memorable creation that trying to find the pieces of the mold from which you chose to be formed would be like trying to find the spark that started the universe.**

You are the artist who has created your product or service, and people always want to "peek behind the curtain" to get a glimpse of the creative process. Imagine if you could ask van Gogh, Renoir, or Monet what they were thinking when they were painting waterlilies, or sunflowers, or any of their famous paintings. To understand what goes on in the mind of the artist makes the artwork even more valuable.

True success has absolutely nothing to do with money or achievement. True success reflects happiness, peace, contentment, serenity, and clarity.

Mercy seems to spread across those who use their adversities to lessen another's. By lessening another's adversity we lessen our own, even retroactively.

The only way to move from rich to enriched, to live a life of purpose and passion, and to ensure that at the end of your life you can look back on a legacy that will cause you and your loved ones to be proud, is to serve others.

If you've been diagnosed with a mental or emotional condition (ADHD, ADD, OCD, ODD, "on the spectrum," etc.) never consider that a barrier to your aspirations. What if you're exactly who you're supposed to be, and you're acting exactly the way that you're supposed to? And what if everything you think is holding you back is designed to help you fulfill your aspirations?

If your aspirations create the road, then legacy is the destination at life's conscious and various end points.

If your profit motive is solely financial,
you can forget ever leaving an enduring legacy.
To create generational success your profit motive must involve
human capital as well—the bettering of human life.

Your highest calling: an otherworldly, burning passion
for the purpose of your life, why you were born.

Work to build your reputation
before you build your bottom line.
You'll find that your ROI
(return on investment) is significantly
enhanced by your ROR
(return on reputation).

My "disorders" have been some of the biggest differentiators in my life, and I'm glad I never was forced to give any of them up by some treatment program or misguided therapist.

The sizzle, the flash: these create intoxication but must be backed up with legacy-leaving substance.

Personal brand intoxication comes from generating surprise and delight in the customer so they are caught off-guard and receptive to the impression you wish to create.

You will undoubtedly run into (and may work with) many people whose credo is to get by rather than do their best. The only way you can ask them to raise their standards is to elevate yours. Demand the best from yourself. You must be the one who sets the example, puts in the work, and takes the responsibility.

You measure net worth by what you have without plunging your bank account nor your soul into debt.

Each one of us is blessed with the ability to succeed not for our sole benefit, but to assist others who will likely not succeed at our level.

I want to always approach life with the same enthusiasm, desire to explore, and wish to grow that young Mickey McKinney had, and if growing up means losing that, then you can count me out.

It's often the second (or third or fourth) act that history regards more ... Is it time for a new act in your life?

What legacy do you aspire to leave behind?

As someone who wants more out of life, you need to start looking for opportunities to do more for others, whether that comes in the form of sharing your gifts of time, talent, or treasure.

I've had thousands of people ask me for the secrets to success. But few of them are willing to put in the work.

Rewriting your own personal history book is within your control. All the mistakes and poor decisions can be annihilated, obliterated, and forgotten.

ERNIE

Your most important legacy won't be the net worth you accumulate but the contributions you make to others. The world should be a better place for you having walked upon it.

Building a legacy is no different than building a house. You do so one brick, one timber, one nail at a time, until the house is finished. You build your legacy one day at a time, one choice at a time.

What's your Mt. Rushmore?
A legacy that will take time to leave?
Stop looking for AI shortcuts, ChatGPT
secrets, or the latest guru to help you
carve it quicker or get there sooner.

Achievements offer you a temporary thrill, a pleasure that initially grows in intensity then turns into pain if you lose the milestone or boredom if you keep it.

Contrary to what your culture, your gurus, and religions have taught you, nothing, but absolutely nothing, can make you happy. Nothing outside of you can bring you lasting joy.

Listen to the images

Legacy

Death

# DEATH Death

**Don't put off living now because you perceive that living then will be better.**

No one should have to sell their soul to comply with societal norms or to make other people happy. There is no price high enough to buy your conformity.

No matter what you believe about what happens after death, one thing's for sure: the greatest gift you have today is your life, right now.

End goals can be a dead end.

MOTHER

Adversity Quotient: The idea that every person on this earth, regardless of the length or circumstances of their life, faces an equal amount of adversity. As with every rule, there are rare exceptions and outliers; however, the adversity that one person experiences is no more severe or debilitating than anyone else's. In this human race, we're all on equal footing.

Far too many people cease to live long before they stop breathing, simply because they stop seeking the next challenge, the next step in their growth.

If you find yourself compromising who you really are, deep down, for any job, relationship, or cause, you should get out immediately.

RANGER

Surely you don't want to arrive at
the final days of your life unscathed,
untouched, untried, untapped.
This would mean that in the end
you will have risked nothing,
tried nothing, done nothing.

Be careful not to mistake self-preservation and self-care for laziness, a self-imposed slow death.

You don't want to take regrets to your grave that sadly came with you due to you not being able to overcome certain fears. Once you overcome those fears, you can accomplish most all of your life's goals and aspirations.

Remember: all things, including your aspirations, come to an end.

MULLIGAN

If I had listened to the naysayers, I would have stayed in Indiana, become a banker, and died of a heart attack at 50 because I hated my life.

Those who are most afraid of dying are often most afraid of living.

Put an end to the person you were born to be to become the person you really want to be.

"Go in peace and be freed from your suffering."

—MARK 5:34

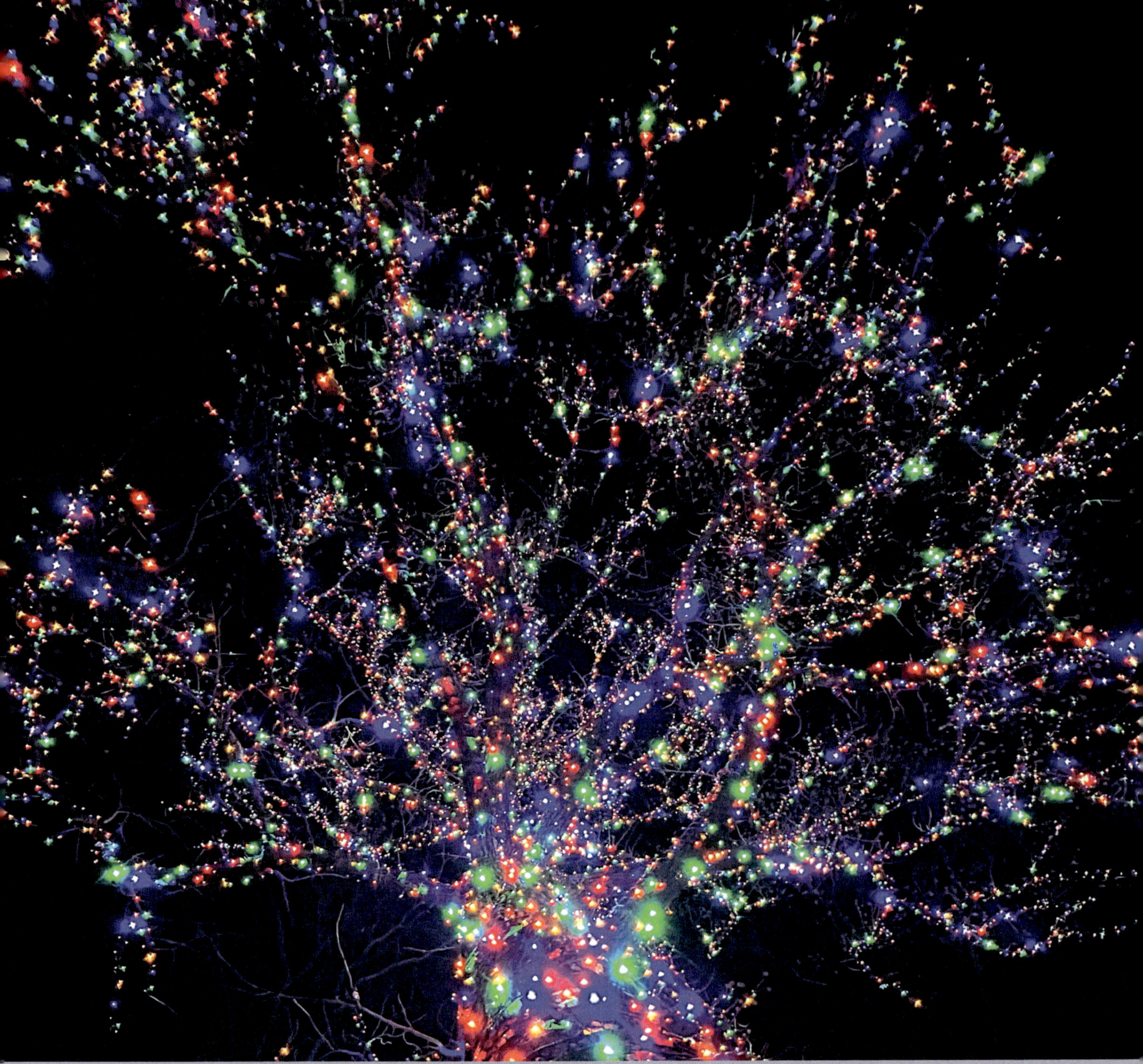

If you want immortality (and we all do),
make it a practice to share your blessings in service
to others and you're likely to have it—in heaven,
if that's your belief, and on earth because people
will remember what you did for them.

Before you die, as often as your mind and body
will allow, pursue the three Is:
the Insurmountable, Incomprehensible,
and Impossible.

FATHER
MOTHER

To live an extraordinary life you must resist an ordinary approach. What is ordinary? It's what most people settle for ... it's a life without purposeful passion, without anything to distinguish it from the billions of other lives on this planet. It's ordinary to depart this world without leaving a mark upon it other than that found on your tombstone. Better yet, leave a scar on the world, not a mark. Marks can be erased; scars are permanent.

Everything, every act, every occurrence
that subtracts from your blessings, your gifts,
your essence was, or will be, self-inflicted.

Once an executioner, always an executioner.

Every time you let fear get in your way,
you're dying a gradual, painful death inside.
When fear stands in your way
(which it will), go around it, over it,
under it, or shove it to the ground.

Listen to the images

Death

40mm FILM 1 A
Risk
1 A FILM 40mm

RISK
Risk

**We experience fear when we start thinking about taking a risk or contemplating taking on a big change or challenge. It's the thought that creates fear—not the risk or challenge itself. Feeling fear is never the problem—letting fear stop you is.**

Purposely smash into the guardrails of life to see if they're real or illusion. If they're real, you find out quickly. But if they're an illusion, breaking through them will be easy, and you'll never be confined by the illusion again.

It's often the uncalculated, unconventional risks that return the greatest rewards.

Badwater

A healthy ego is based upon a combination of three elements. First is exuberance—a greater-than-normal, bubbling-over, otherworldly and extraordinary passion for your purpose. Second is a belief that you are one of the best in the world at what you do. Third is a lack of fear about sharing your belief and passion with the world. You're on the earth with 8,000,000,000 people. If you're not boiling over with passion for your purpose, if you're not supremely confident in yourself and your abilities, and if you're not willing to share that with the world, how will you ever stand out and be found, much less recognized and ultimately remembered?

DRINK
VAIN

Riches, excitement, and enlightenment are rarely found by following the marked exits on the highway of life. Instead, you need to seek the obscure, dark, scary, and remote paths that few people dare to follow.

I don't care who you are, how happy or successful you've been, how many people praise you to the skies, how many businesses you've built, charities you've helped, or lives you've transformed … there always will be parts of your inner life, places found only in the deep recesses of your soul, that will make you want to run screaming into the night.

Taking your own personal moonshot involves risks.
Sure, the progress that you have made has been incremental,
alternating between 2 steps forward, 1.98 steps back,
and 2 steps back and 1.99 steps forward, inching along ...
but it's time to shake off being so methodical.

Never compromise on your artistic vision.

HOW TO
CREATE
YOUR OWN
REALITY
AND
FOR LEASE

## Risk Continuum

**Phobic** **Daredevil**

*Determine where you fall on the risk threshold continuum.*

If you're closer to phobic than daredevil,
it's time to exercise your risk threshold.

Say yes to small opportunities.

When you're ready, say yes to larger ones.

Everyone falls somewhere between these two extremes.

Where do you fall?

You're not going to change until you let go of your attachments. An attachment is an emotional clinging caused by your belief that without something or someone you cannot be happy. I know: easier said than done. But until you release your attachment(s), all your efforts to change will result only in you changing your behavior, not yourself. And once you've released your attachments you really don't change. You don't have to. You are then free to redirect behavior or thoughts that were self-destructive into something constructive, or reignite something that was inside you all along.

Redirect. Reignite. Rewire!

You'll never break free from that which constrains you unless you're willing to risk failure to test the strength of your perceived bondage.

Risk is the ultimate performance-enhancing supplement.
Risk increases adrenaline while also increasing
your opportunity for greater reward.

Don't settle for reform when what is needed is revolt.

We need to bring back a little more of that teenage focus
on the emotional rewards of risk and tell the prefrontal cortex—
the part of the brain that is acting "parental"—
to shut the f— — — up.

"Don't be afraid, just believe."

—Mark 5:36

Some of the best deals I've made are the ones I've walked away from.

The three Rs: Responsible Risk = Rewards.

N5793

I was scared enough to educate myself.

I'm a daredevil—maybe so. But I'm no fool. I believe in taking risks, but I also believe in study, practice, starting small, and making gradual progress.

CAI
EXW 10 - 8
EW 9 - 7
IL 50 - 6
IW 9 - 6
IH 11 - 1
CUFT 5347
H 13 - 3
H 14 - 10
2 INCH TREAD COND. SHOES

R.I.S.K. Requires Intense Self-Knowledge

Don't let the "risk" pendulum swing too far
toward caution and consequences, and away from excitement,
anticipation, and action.

When you use fear as a signal to move forward
rather than retreat, making the decision
to take the risk is easier.

MANDATORY
EVACUATION
ZONE
ROAD CLOSED
CITY OF DELRAY BEACH

Dust off your leather bag of tools and get to work!
Two simple things that this guy with a 1.8 GPA and seven stints in juvenile detention did: took incremental then enormous risks and worked daily until they paid off big time.

Whether your aspirations are physical, financial, spiritual, entrepreneurial, relational, emotional, dietary, or professional, you must boldly face your fears and take risks, even when it scares the sh*t out of you.

Scared means something different to me:
a sensation resulting from the pursuit of an opportunity.

Listen to the images

Risk

Hope

HOPE
Hope

**I'm a pathological optimist.
Try it on; it'll look good on you.**

**Right now, in this very moment,
it's as good as it gets.
Oh, it's gonna get better,
but now is as good as it gets.**

Aspiration: Having that otherworldly desire
to achieve something high and great ....

I believe each one of us has a bright star inside
just waiting for that supernova event, ready to break out
of the idea of who we are "supposed" to be so we can
reinvent and re-create who we truly want to be.

Every day we have a chance to better our previous best,
a chance to change the mind of fate itself.

I share these images and thoughts of aspiration, of hope, of faith, of success in life, so that you know that you're not alone. Today, I simply want to share how grateful I am. You see, behind the smiling and uplifting writings there can be a deep, sometimes dark, struggle. I'm grateful for the awareness and deep faith that has allowed me to endure, and, in the end, prevail. I'm smiling because I'm a happy and optimistic guy. And I'm happy because I'm grateful for the discernment to always see hope at the other end of "never quit." No, I'm not always the positive person that it seems, but I am positive in my belief that tomorrow, as sure as the sun rises, so dawns a new day of hope—always and without fail.

What follows hope realized? What state are you in when hope succeeds, bears fruit, materializes? Think about that ...

Get the mind right and the money will follow.

I'm not a fan of long-term planning;
I don't go out more than a year
for anything that I plan.

Charity exacerbates poverty. Philanthro-capitalism solves it.
With philanthro-capitalism, capital is measured in human
rather than financial terms.

I'm not looking for a new normal;
instead, I want a more frequent extraordinary.
And that doesn't just happen with the
changing of a profile picture.

Get off your knees and pray walking.
Say your prayers while in motion.

Sometimes I struggle with what most find easy
and find easy what most struggle with.

The energy and emotion you put into pursuing
and obtaining material things are never returned to you
with the same intensity once you possess the thing.

It's OK to believe fully now.
Let all that hesitation go.

Seeing the world through rose-colored glasses
means you have an optimistic perception of something,
a positive opinion, seeing something in a positive way.
In short, it means you have favorably disposed
opinions and optimistic "eyes."
So what's wrong with that?

Mindset precedes results every time.
Producing results reinforces the mindset that will
put you on the path of realizing the aspirations
that give your life meaning and purpose.

FRESH
EGGS $4

Never be one for the "averages," "medians" or "means" in life ... always look at the outliers, those possibilities at the fringe of impossible.

Any wall or barrier that is self-created can also be torn down or broken out of. Be willing to give up one part of your identity to be reborn as a new, better version of yourself.

Within the four corners of a book is a small business that all authors hope turns into a big business.

"Father, if you are willing, please take this cup of suffering away from me. Yet I want your will to be done, not mine." Jesus spoke these enlightened words right before he was arrested on the Mount of Olives and led off to be crucified on what is now known as Good Friday. We also often ask God, or whomever or whatever we cry out to, to remove our suffering and adversities. But notice how quickly Jesus moves from denial to acceptance. When faced with adversity, whether innocent or consequential, the sooner we accept it the sooner we can find our own salvation from denial, blame, anger, or resentment. And finally, when Jesus had uttered these words, the following passage was entered into the gospel of Luke: "Then, an angel from heaven appeared to him and strengthened him." You are never alone on your Mount of Olives, your Road to Cavalry. There is always a Simon to help bear your cross, an angel waiting to lift you up on her wings. Just look around you. You'll find them.

I'm just the opening act for the main performance, which is the experience people have when they walk through the front door of the most beautiful oceanfront home they've ever seen.

Celebrate each humble victory as a triumphant achievement. This builds confidence and, like the momentum of a flywheel, confidence allows us to get our minds right so the (money, miles, relationships, aspirations, etc.) will follow.

Balance the drive to better your previous best
with the ability to enjoy your accomplishments as you go.

Relentless Forward Motion: With relentless forward motion,
a spirit full of life and adventure, and a willingness
to embrace risk, anything and everything is possible.

Be a lifelong learner, not a lifelong student.
Learners apply what they know;
students never leave the classroom.

Listen to the images

Hope

GOD
God

**Since free will is a gift from God, use it to honor the giver.**

**There really is no "bad" or "good," just gifts from God that come in glittering, well-wrapped packages with a red bow, or ugly and torn shoeboxes that are held together with duct tape and a tattered grocery bag. Either way, they are gifts. Learn to enjoy both.**

I don't care if you're a Christian, Muslim, Jew, Hindu, Buddhist, atheist, agnostic, or none of the above, and it doesn't matter to me if you read the Bible or the Koran or the Talmud or *People* magazine, or fortune cookies. I believe that regardless of faith (or lack of it), most of us at some point close our eyes and send up a prayer to whatever we call God, to ask either for blessings for ourselves and those we love, or relief from a problem. If we inventory our prayers, they all come down to simply asking for more.

More health. More wealth. More love.

More happiness. More peace.

CHURCH
ENTRANCE

Share what you have, regardless of how much you possess. Start now and start small if you must. Don't let excuses like "I don't have time," "I'm not rich," or "What difference am I going to make?" get in your way.

Regardless of the debilitating moments we face in our business, health, personal life, relationships, etc., if we just allow the passage of time and faith in God to cure the ailment, we will soon emerge triumphant.

God *always* answers a sincere prayer.
It may not happen in the way that you initially asked
or as soon as you'd like ...
but an answer always comes.
God is tapping you, calling you,
prodding you to find a way to redefine
what you want so that it has meaning to
someone other than you alone.
Stay open to the unforeseen ways
in which God may deliver
exactly what you need.

Move from rich to enriched. It's clear to me that the secret of moving from rich to enriched is simple: become a responsible steward for the blessings you receive, no matter how small or large.

You see yourself as "chosen," not because you have some superior genetics or are more special than another, but because you have stepped up and said to God, "Yes, please. I can handle the mine fields. I am a responsible steward of all the blessings you have in store for me."

Dovetail your professional highest calling with your spiritual highest calling.

"To whom much is given,
much is required."

—Luke 12:48

God: I've loved you since the moment you were born. I've followed your every footstep, every stumble, stride, and shuffle. Every victory and every loss. I shared them all with you. I've always been here, ready for you to seek me and ask for my grace, my mercy, my forgiveness.

In our pleas to God, are we pleasing God?

The only way to return to the gifts that God has given you is to turn from the things that are stealing them away from you.

"Be sure to show hospitality to strangers,
for by doing so some have shown hospitality
to angels without knowing it."

— Hebrews 13:2

Make your prayer today the same as King Solomon's prayer,
the richest person in history ($2.1 trillion in today's dollars):
for a discerning and enlightened heart.

The moment when things start to look most difficult
is the time to get most excited about God's coming tap.

Nature is God.
God is nature.

The devil covets those closest to God.
Life's minefields become more concentrated
as you succeed in enlarging your territory for God.
Be hyper-careful where you step as you ascend.

God tests. The devil tempts.
When tempted, don't say, *God is tempting me.*

"Resist the devil, and he will flee from you."

—JAMES 4:7

HOLY
BIBLE
LUKE 19:30
581
LUKE 7:19
571
PSALM 103:10
LUKE 5:2
569
LUKE 2:30
567
The Birth of Jesus

If your Bible is falling apart,
your life probably isn't.

God doesn't respect the boundaries we fabricate to separate the spiritual and the secular. God is just as likely to tap you while you're in line at 7-Eleven or Walmart as at some magnificent church on a hilltop.

JESUS I TRUST
IN YOU

There are special points in time when the divine hand
lightly makes contact with the mortal self,
and we're given a choice: action or denial,
sharing or selfishness, evolving or staying
within the confines of the familiar.

There is no on-off switch for spirit.
You allow it to infuse your life
with the wonder and will of God.

Listen to the images

God

LOVE
Love

**When one tries to describe love, you really can't. It's like trying to describe the color red to someone without sight or the flavor of a mango to someone who's never tasted one.**

When the heart speaks the mind has no choice but to listen then act. When the rational mind speaks the heart fights but eventually (and sadly) is often silenced.
Unlike the mind, the heart is incapable of comprehending mental, societal, or moral conventions, limitations, and boundaries.
So goes the beautiful, irrational conflict ... Stay irrational.

Start satisfying others' unmet needs and see how quickly this increases your awareness of what you need.

The higher you go during your rapid rate of ascent,
the fewer people you will encounter in that same sphere.
So surround yourself with those you trust,
and learn to love your own company.

It's never the gifts of jewelry, fancy clothes, or exotic trips that cause a relationship to thrive. Instead, it's the smallest reflections of love and the random reminders of affection that keep the diamond of your relationship polished and shining brightly.

Once you are able to love yourself,
don't hesitate to let others know.

To set the stage for mind-blowing sex, it's important to engage in what I call fore-foreplay. The three most important aspects of fore-foreplay are thoughtfulness, appreciation, and sensuality.

Charisma is like fireworks: you are enthralled by the show, but once it's over, you go home—you're not going to keep staring at the sky. Magnetic-ism is like looking at the northern lights: they go on and on, deeper and deeper, swirling as they become more brilliant and enthralling. You want to be around that person because there's always more to see and discover.

The best mind-blowing sex completely turns the mind off.

Personal brand intoxication occurs when you have the heightened attention of every single one of the customer's senses to the point where there is a momentary lapse of concentration in the mind and breath in the lungs. It's in these moments of intoxication that your personal brand becomes fixed in people's minds and elevated beyond that of any competitor. This intoxication is involuntary and usually subliminal, meaning that it isn't something the customer went in looking for or expecting.

It's more like an evening where you are enjoying a great bottle of wine. As you savor one glass after another, there's a slow buildup of sensual overwhelm and you aren't aware of how intoxicated you're becoming. That's the kind of experience you want to create for your customers. You want them gradually to fall so in love with you and your brand that they cannot imagine doing business with anyone else.

Grace, mercy, love, forgiveness, and redemption abound when one asks sincerely and with repentance.

Move from falling in love to being in love. Whatever you do, find love.

I can't possibly overstate how especially important the support and encouragement of your significant other is to your self-confidence and, therefore, the success of your life's ventures. Whether your partner in life is also a partner in your profession or not, he or she is like the crew chief for your Badwater 135-mile ultramarathon, in that this person deeply affects your ability to bring your best to each contest. I've watched some mediocre players rise to the height of their abilities because they had someone in their corner who always wanted the best for and from them, but I've also watched many people's promising careers tank in the wake of an unsupportive spouse or life partner. (Yes, Nilsa has been my "crew chief" for all 12 of my Badwater ultramarathon races!)

You and your significant other should be like the two rails of a railroad track: separate and equidistant from each other, but always heading in the same direction.

Mind-blowing sex is a sensual dance between love and lust: love sweetens and deepens the connection between you two, and lust fans the flames of passion and takes both partners over the edge to completion.

Marry your guardian angel.

You should always seek to give mind-blowing sex, not *have* mind-blowing sex. "Have" can be selfish; "give" means that you firmly (pun intended) place your partner's pleasure and satisfaction at the forefront of your mind, often ahead of your own desires.

"I've always seen every line of Proverbs 31:10-31
as describing you, Nilsa.
You are that wife, that gift, that treasure."
If you're a woman, strive to be a Proverbs 31 woman.

Guys, take your man-pill
and do what must be done.

Diamonds are formed 90 miles below the earth's surface, in upwards of 725,000 pounds of pressure per square inch and at temperatures of at least 2,000 degrees Fahrenheit. Most minerals crumble or liquefy under such extreme circumstances. It's the same with relationships: most of them can't withstand even small amounts of emotional stress, pressure, and heat. Whether the conflict in your relationship produces divorce or diamonds all depends on you and your significant other's approach to pressure.

Relationship pressure creates diamonds.

In your relationships (intimate or friendly), do you concentrate on who gives what and how much? Or are you so happy to be with this person that all you want to do is give him or her everything you possibly can? Scorekeeping diminishes relationships.

Fall in love: Don't hesitate to show your affection. Don't hesitate on anything! Falling in love is one of the greatest experiences we can have. And I'm not just talking romantically. We can love our friends, our kids, our hobbies, charities, and communities.

If a little is good, a lot is better.

It is enormously powerful when a guardian angel's love is so deep that it causes the other person to alter his or her free will.

Take an artist's approach to your craft.

The word *passion* is tossed around like a rag doll. I believe that passion occurs when something lays itself on your heart to such a degree that it drops your blood pressure, raises your heart rate, and aligns with your true purpose.

Listen to the images

Love

# ACKNOWLEDGMENTS

First, I acknowledge God and the gifts He has entrusted to me. In total there are 32 references to God in ***Aspirational Thoughts* • *Inspirational Images*.** One of the quotes reads, "Since free will is a gift from God, use it to honor the giver." I hope I did so.

Within the four corners of a book is a small business that all authors hope turns into a big business. (Sound familiar?) No small business ever turns into a successful big business without help, without collaboration.

Truth be told, I have never put together a jigsaw puzzle on my own, nor did I compile *Aspirational Thoughts* • *Inspirational Images* by myself.

This monumental undertaking took the better part of a year that involved an astounding team of enigmatologists and cruciverbalists. (Sorry, you gotta look 'em up.)

I begin by thanking **Robert Mott** of RobertMottDesigns.com for not only designing the cover and interior of the book you're holding, but also for helping me meticulously place the right quotes with the perfect photos. Robert also produced the original graphics and trailer video that came out on January 24, 2024 for the book. (If you haven't seen the vid yet, head over to my social media or YouTube channel and scroll to that date.) We spent hundreds of hours in each other's heads. Unless you're an author or book designer, it's hard to comprehend how much goes into the design of the exterior and interior of a book, all the way down to the detail found at the beginning on that "Library of Congress" copyright page that no one reads. I can assure you, without a beautiful and well-thought-out design, your reading experience wouldn't be what it is (or was).

There is no way I could have cut down 1,112 thoughts and quotes to the 261 that made the final cut without **Julie McCarron**. Julie was a second set of eyes that also went back and read through my prior books, social media posts, and webpages and helped me discard the puzzle pieces that didn't quite fit. Don't worry, I didn't throw them away permanently; there's always the next book.

*You mean the world to me* is how I started an email to **Karen Risch Mott** in early 2024 as I asked (begged) her to help me copyedit this book. Karen has been by my side for the better part of 20 years, through all eight of my books. Heck, she has organized prior book tours, helped with Audible recordings, and even crewed for me at one of my Badwater 135-mile ultramarathon races in Death Valley, California—in 130-degree heat! She currently holds a prestigious position at James Madison University that no longer affords her the time to work on the complex and tedious process of putting a book together. What made copyediting this book so difficult is that the writing style is more poetic in nature, meaning it contains far less structure and far more "riff." How do you copyedit a book that doesn't comply with convention? You beg the best collaborator in the history of history while on your knees.

If you work with me, I expect you to be able to wear many hats. **Leslie Barrett** had to buy a bigger hat rack! Not only did Leslie help refine the best of the best quotes, but she also proofread the book multiple times. She is the brains behind the upcoming 25-state, 35-city, 50-venue, 60-day, near 10,000-mile *Aspirational Thoughts • Inspirational Images* Book Tour. This two-month odyssey will stop in cities and states up the East Coast then through the Midwest, turn north and hug the northern states all the way to Washington, then cut diagonally to finish back in Florida. Talk about putting together the pieces of a jigsaw puzzle! Leslie will schedule all the stops at over 50+/- homeless shelters, soup kitchens, food pantries, veterans' facilities, abused women's shelters, juvenile detention centers, schools, art galleries, hospitals, TV stations, radio stations, podcasts, and bookstores to deliver the messages of hope found in this book.

Speaking of the *Aspirational Thoughts • Inspirational Images* Book Tour, once again **"Holy" Juan Restrepo**, the "Juan and Only," will join me for every one of those 10,000 miles. Juan is a 20-year Caring House Project Board of Directors member who has driven the tour buses and provided the digital media for my book tours dating back to my book *The Tap* 15 years ago. Juan will not only drive all those miles; he will selflessly help carry our book posters, books, and media equipment into all 50+ venues. He'll set up and coordinate everything in advance with our hosts. Imagine being cooped up with me for what will now total 30,000+ miles!

If you followed the cryptic and suspenseful creation of the reveal for this book, its eventual release, and all the media coverage chronicled, you've undoubtedly visited AT-II.com or AspirationalThoughts.com. That "Disney on a desktop" page was created by the hyper-talented Master of Media Mayhem, **Brian Kay** of BrianKayDesigns.com.

Were you there for the book's reveal stunt on Leap Day 2024 or the release party on 4.24.24? While the stunt seemed to upset the police (for once, seeking forgiveness instead of permission didn't work), and **Sarah Martin** of Experience Epic had nothing to do with the reveal that nearly landed me in jail, she did plan the dramatic, immersive, captivating, and theatrical book launch event at the Boca Raton Museum of Art. Thank you Sarah and team for such a memorable and jaw-dropping spectacle.

Finally, I'm saving the best for last. Would there even have been an *Aspirational Thoughts • Inspirational Images* book without my wife, **Nilsa,** or my daughter, **Laura**? No freaking way. One of the more humorous quotes from the Laugh chapter of the book reads, "I believe that had God not sent Nilsa to me I'd likely be dead or living in a beat-up old Airstream trailer somewhere in the backwoods of West Virginia, wearing overalls, chewing tobacco, smelling like motor oil, and married to the bearded lady from the circus." That kind of says it all about the significance of Nilsa in my life. My daughter, Laura, is and always will be daddy's little girl. Although she is 25 years old, has her mommy's looks and her dad's height, lives in New York City, and has her own business (StrataBrand), she has a brilliant marketing mind. Every single marketing decision I made was first concocted with and collaborated on with Laura. I love her dearly and am so proud of her.

What about you, the reader? Yes, I thank you and acknowledge you for wanting to better yourself and the lives of those you love by reading and sharing in the life-enhancing adventure known as *Aspirational Thoughts • Inspirational Images*.

## ABOUT FRANK MCKINNEY

Frank McKinney is a true modern-day Renaissance man who has redefined the limits of success through his every endeavor.

His early years were not very promising, however: he spent seven stints in juvenile detention, and, upon attending his fourth high school in four years, as he was asked to leave the first three, he earned his high school diploma with a 1.8 GPA. (It would have been lower, but he received an A in creative writing.)

So, with $50 in his pocket and without the benefit of further education, Frank left his native Indiana for Florida in search of his highest calling. Today, Frank's life is a testament to the power of aspirational thinking, inspirational imaging, and the ability to create a completely new reality. As a real estate artist, he has created and sold 44 oceanfront mansions on speculation, with an average selling price of $14 million. As a philanthro-capitalist, he has built 32 self-sustaining villages in Haiti over the last 22 years, providing more than

14,400 children and their families with homes, renewable food, clean water, and the means to support themselves. A bestselling author, actor, photographer, and keynote speaker, he has now written nine books in eight genres, starred in four movies, and keynoted before audiences of 10 to 10,000 around the world. Physically, Frank has pushed the limits of his body by racing in the Badwater 135-mile ultramarathon 12 times in the scorching 130-degree summer in Death Valley, California, a race referred to by *National Geographic* as "the world's toughest footrace." Will there be a lucky 13th?

Frank believes you need a unique space or place to draw out creativity and ingenuity. He wrote *Aspirational Thoughts • Inspirational Images* from his one-of-a-kind glass treehouse cabin along the Pigeon River in Canton, North Carolina.

Today, Frank and his wife, Nilsa, split their time between their home in South Florida and their glass cabin along the river. They enjoy visiting their daughter, Laura, in New York City, where she started and runs StrataBrand, a brand strategy firm.

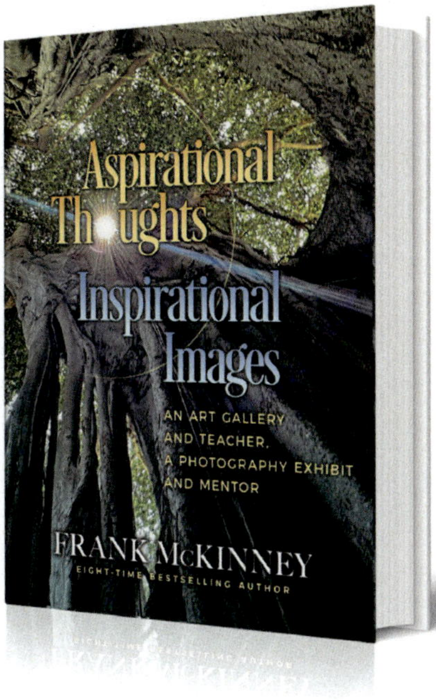


Share the beauty and wonderment of

# Aspirational Thoughts Inspirational Images

**Give copies of**
***Aspirational Thoughts • Inspirational Images***
**to family, friends and co-workers …**

Hardcover (Caring House Books, 2024)
Available on Amazon or AspirationalThoughts.com

## OTHER BESTSELLING OFFERINGS FROM FRANK McKINNEY

***Adversitology: Overcoming Adversity When You're Hanging on by a Thread***

*Adversitology* is part inspirational memoir and part "how to" handbook for dealing with life's big and small challenges. Reach for it: Your lifeline is in front of you …

What if this book is the lifeline you need?

Let's face it: adversity is an unavoidable part of every life. Serious trouble comes for all of us, threatening to ruin our finances, physical and mental health, or relationships. And if you've ever felt as if you were barely hanging on while dealing with something big …

***You're not alone …***

Paperback, hardcover, Audible, Kindle, and autographed (Caring House Books, 2023)

Available at Adversitology.com • $25

***Aspire! How to Create Your Own Reality and Alter Your DNA*** asks, "Can you really create your own reality and alter your DNA?" Real estate artist and bestselling author Frank McKinney has done just that. He's pushed the limits professionally (creating then selling 44 multimillion-dollar oceanfront mansions on spec), philanthropically (building 32 self-sustaining villages in the poorest country on earth), creatively (writing nine books in eight genres), and physically (running the Badwater 135-mile ultramarathon 12 times).

Paperback, hardcover, Audible, Kindle, and autographed (Caring House Books, 2021) • Available at TheAspireBook.com • $30.00

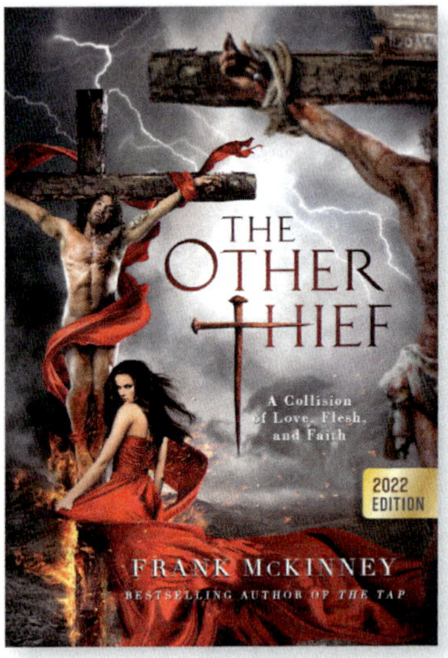


***The Other Thief*** is a controversial, heart-wrenching novel of deception, pride, and lust, along with mercy, grace, forgiveness, and—above all—love. Frank McKinney boldly enters the Christian romance genre with this seductively spiritual novel. *The Other Thief* will arouse readers and their faith, leaving them wondering which side of the cross they would choose.

Hardcover (HCI, 2018)
Available at TheOtherThief.com • $20

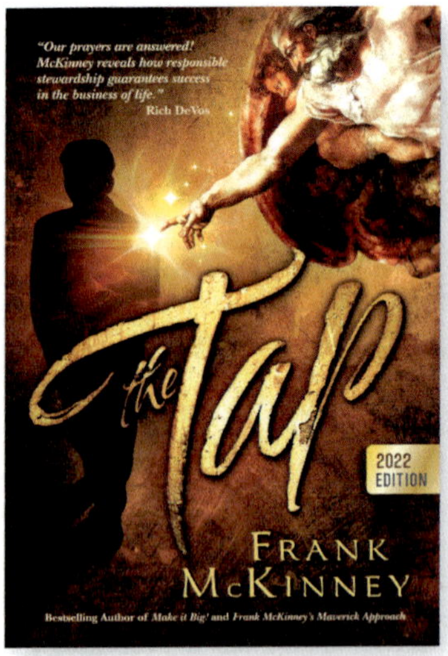


Bestselling author Frank McKinney introduces ***The Tap,*** a profound spiritual practice leading to success in the business of life. Your prayers for more are answered! *The Tap* shows how to sensitize yourself to feel and then act on life's great "Tap Moments," embracing the rewards and responsibilities of a blessed life. Feel it, follow it, and find your highest calling. This book is about accepting responsibility, and it gives you confidence in your ability to handle your "more," whether it's more wealth, health, happiness, or relationships.

Hardcover (HCI, 2009) • Available at The-Tap.com • $25

***Burst This! Frank McKinney's Bubble-Proof Real Estate Strategies*** continues Frank's international bestselling tradition of delivering paradoxical perspectives and strategies for generational success in real estate. Tired of all the "bubble" talk, all the doom and gloom? Here comes McKinney in his unassailable fear-removal gear to help you wash away the worry—the anxiety that financial theorists and misguided media constantly dump into the real estate marketplace. During his decades-long career, this "maverick daredevil real estate artist" has not only survived but thrived through all economic conditions by taking the contrarian position and making his own real estate markets.

Hardcover (HCI, 2009) • Available at Burst-This.com • $30

---

With ***Dead Fred, Flying Lunchboxes and the Good Luck Circle,*** Frank McKinney boldly enters young reader fiction with this fantasy novel charged with fairy-tale wonder, enthralling magic, page-turning suspense, and the deep creativity he's known for. It will both race and gladden the hearts of readers of all ages. This classic was inspired by real-life Laura McKinney's 1,652 walks to school with her friends and her father, Frank McKinney.

Hardcover (HCI, 2009)
Available at Dead-Fred.com • $25

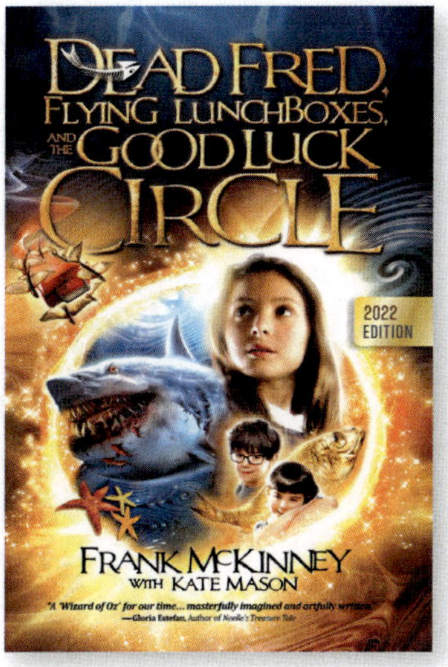

***Frank McKinney's Maverick Approach to Real Estate Success*** takes the reader on a fascinating real estate odyssey that began more than three decades ago with a $50,000 fixer-upper and culminates in $100 million mansion. Includes strategies and insights from a true real estate "artist," visionary, and market maker.

Paperback (John Wiley & Sons, 2006)
Available at Frank-McKinney.com • $25

---

***Make It BIG! 49 Secrets for Building a Life of Extreme Success,*** Frank's first book consists of 49 short, dynamic chapters that share how to live a life full of meaning and purpose, with real estate stories and "deal points" sprinkled throughout.

Hardcover (John Wiley & Sons, 2002)
Available at Frank-McKinney.com • $30

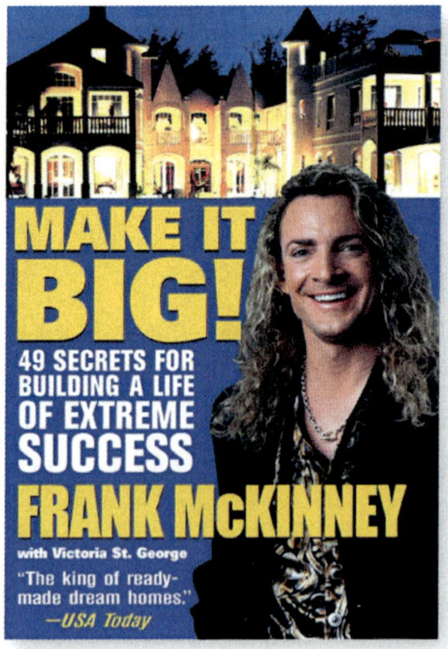

**The Frank McKinney Experience, Keynotes, Appearances, Personal "Aspirational Thoughts" Coaching**

One-on-one or group events and bulk pricing.

Inquire: Pamela@Frank-McKinney.com

**Please visit Frank-McKinney.com,** which has been referred to as "Disney on a Desktop" by *PCMag,* for all things Frank McKinney! Proceeds from the sale of *Aspirational Thoughts • Inspirational Images* and all of Frank's books benefit his Caring House Project Foundation (CHPF). To learn more about CHPF and its 32 self-sustaining villages built in Haiti over the last 22 years, providing 14,400 children and their families with homes, renewable food, clean water, and the means to support themselves, visit CHPF.org.

Caring House

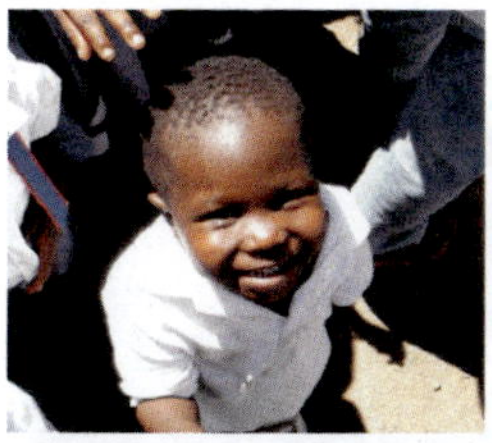

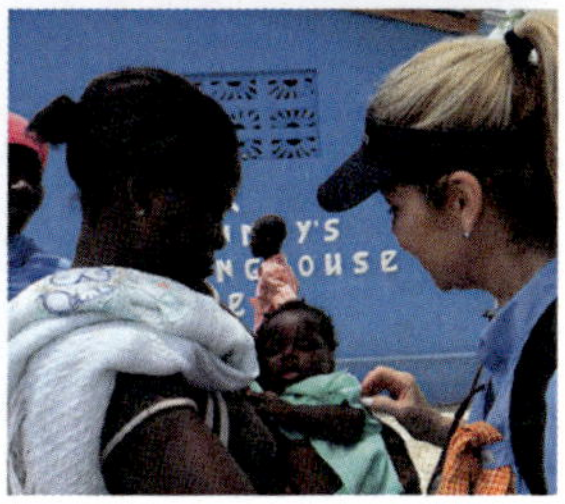

frank.mckinney.10

FrankMcKinney1

thefrankmckinney

frankmckinney

frankmckinneyauthor

frankmckinney

frank-mckinney.com

Made in the USA
Monee, IL
12 April 2024

59f5a8a9-3e7e-4128-9b5c-436fc618146fR02